OUR LIVING WORLD: EARTH'S BIOMES

Rivers, Streams, Lakes, and Ponds

Barbara A. Somervill

TRADITION BOOKS®, MAPLE PLAIN, MINNESOTA

A NEW TRADITION IN CHILDREN'S PUBLISHING™

volume 3

Rivers, Streams, Lakes, and Ponds

ABOUT THE AUTHOR

Barbara A. Somervill is the author

of many books for children. She loves

learning and sees every writing

project as a chance to learn new

information or gain a new under-

standing. Ms. Somervill grew up in

New York State, but has also lived in

Toronto, Canada; Canberra, Australia;

California; and South Carolina. She

currently lives with her husband in

Simpsonville, South Carolina.

CONTENT ADVISER

Susan Woodward, Professor of

Geography, Radford University,

Radford, Virginia

In gratitude to George R. Peterson Sr. for introducing me to the beauty of creation
—George R. Peterson Jr., Publisher, Tradition Books®

Published in the United States of America by Tradition Books® and distributed to the school
and library market by The Child's World®

[ACKNOWLEDGMENTS]
For Editorial Directions, Inc.: E. Russell Primm, Editorial Director; Dana Meachen Rau, Line
Editor; Katie Marsico, Associate Editor; Judi Shiffer, Associate Editor and Library Media
Specialist; Matthew Messbarger, Editorial Assistant; Susan Hindman, Copy Editor; Lucia
Raatma, Proofreaders; Ann Grau Duvall, Peter Garnham, Deborah Grahame, Katie
Marsico, Elizabeth K. Martin, and Kathy Stevenson, Fact Checkers; Tim Griffin/IndexServ,
Indexer; Cian Loughlin O'Day, Photo Researcher; Linda S. Koutris, Photo Selector

For The Design Lab: Kathleen Petelinsek, design, art direction, and cartography;
Kari Thornborough, page production

[PHOTOS]
Cover/frontispiece: Steve Austin; Papilio/Corbis.
Interior: Animals Animals/Earth Scenes: 24 (Victoria McCormick), 35 (Erwin & Peggy Bauer),
43 (Phil Degginger), 51 (Carmela Leszczynski); Darren Bennett/Animals Animals/Earth
Scenes: 5, 30; Corbis: 10 (David Muench), 11 (James Amos), 14 (Rob Howard), 33 (Charles
Krebs), 34 (Lynda Richardson), 36 (Jay Dickman), 44 (Tom Brakefield), 53 (Niall Benvie), 56
(Joe McDonald), 57, 59 (Terry Eggers), 61 (Raymond Gehman), 66 (Chris Hellier), 67 (Stuart
Westmorland), 68 (Paul A. Souders), 71 (Brandon D. Cole), 73 (Staffan Widstrand), 80 (Theo
Allofs), 82 (Bettmann), 83 (Galen Rowell), 86 (Charles E. Rotkin), 87 (Julia Waterlow; Eye
Ubiquitous), 90 (Angelo Hornak), 91 (John Henley); Digital Vision: 41, 62, 85; Ecoscene/
Corbis: 4 (Andrew Brown), 79 (Joel Creed); Frank Lane Picture Agency/Corbis: 27 (Douglas P.
Wilson), 49 (B. Borrell Casal), 55 (Tony Wharton); Getty Images/Brand X Pictures: 6, 7, 8,
12, 40, 65; Getty Images/The Image Bank/Davies & Starr: 45; François Gohier: 74; Randall
Hyman: 75, 76; Dwight R. Kuhn: 39, 52; Frans Lanting/Minden Pictures: 63; Mary McDonald/
Naturepl.com: 50; Gary Meszaros/Dembinsky Photo Associates: 48, 88; Photodisc: 20, 29, 31,
32, 70; Douglas Stamm: 54; Tom Stack & Associates: 28 (Tom & Therisa Stack), 46 (Tom
Stack), 60 (Doug Sokell), 72 (Jeff Foott).

[LIBRARY OF CONGRESS CATALOGING-IN-PUBLICATION DATA]
CIP data available

Table of Contents

[Chapter One]

Defining Rivers, Streams, Lakes, and Ponds

The spring thaw releases water that has been bound up in ice and snow. Water trickles down a Rocky Mountain hillside. The trickle feeds a rushing stream. The stream swells a lake. Excess lake water pours into Colorado's South Platte River. Each spring, water

▲ Cutthroat trout like this one nearly became extinct in Colorado's lakes and streams.

moves across the land, renewing waterways.

Fresh, flowing water is essential for the survival of the greenback cutthroat trout. The species is **native** to Colorado's mountain streams.

Once, greenback cutthroat trout faced **extinction**. A government program changed the cutthroat trout's fate. The program cleaned up streams and reduced the use of rivers by industries. The trout could breed and recover its normal population numbers. Today, greenback cutthroat trout swim in more than 40 Colorado lakes and streams.

The Water Cycle

🦎 Water covers nearly three-fourths of earth. Yet very little of that water

◀ A Colorado stream pours down a slope in the Rocky Mountains.

? WORDS TO KNOW . . .

biomes (BYE-ohmz) large ecosystems in which the plants and animals are adapted to a particular climate or physical environment

groundwater (ground-WAW-tur) water that exists in bedrock below the surface of the earth

is fresh. Just more than 97 percent of earth's water lies in oceans and seas. It is salt water and is not suitable for drinking.

Freshwater is limited to less than 3 percent of earth's water supply. Glaciers and icebergs hold two-thirds of that ice in water. About three-fifths of 1 percent is **groundwater.** And less than one-fifth of 1 percent fills rivers and lakes. Freshwater **biomes** include lakes, ponds, puddles, rivers, streams, and seeps (which are small springs).

There is no "new" water. There is only water that has been recycled in hundreds of ways, thousands of times. Water, then, moves through a cycle over long periods of time. A single drop of water in the ocean may become water vapor and rise into the air. Later, it

◄ Glaciers like this one in Antarctica hold about 2 percent of the earth's water.

▲ Snowmelt fills mountain streams each spring.

may fall onto the earth as rain or snow. Water drops may mix with salt. They can be frozen and thawed. Water may even pass through the human body. It is then cleaned naturally or at a water treatment plant. Then it returns to the ground and reenters the water cycle.

Rivers and Streams

🐇 Melted snow, rain, or **runoff** travels downhill.

✋ DO IT!

Are you a water waster? Look for ways to waste less water. Take shorter showers. Use cooled cooking water to water garden plants. Do not let the faucet run while you brush your teeth. Fill the kitchen sink with water to rinse dishes, glasses, and utensils.

❓ WORDS TO KNOW . . .

runoff (RUHN-awf) water that travels over the ground

▲ Rivers cut narrow gorges through dense woodland.

Rivers and streams are moving freshwater. Streams often begin in mountains, on hillsides, or in underground springs. Runoff water collects into a stream. The stream feeds a river. The difference between a stream and a river is the amount of water it carries. Rivers carry more water than streams. When one river feeds another, it is called a tributary.

A river's age determines its flow. A younger river has fast-paced water. It cuts a straighter path through the ground and rock than an older river. Fast-moving water erodes, or grinds away, rock and soil.

Older rivers wander along their routes. As the river erodes its banks, its path

Water goes wherever it flows most easily. Cracks in rocks and dips in the ground create routes for running water.

changes from straight to curvy. The curves are called meanders. A very old river has many meanders. The more a river curves, the slower it moves.

Look at a map of the Mississippi River, the longest river in the United States. The Mississippi begins as a small stream at Lake Itasca,

▲ The Mississippi River's watershed, or drainage area, along with several of its tributaries

▲ This peaceful lake forms the headwaters of the mighty Mississippi River.

Missouri, the Ohio, and the Red rivers. By the time it reaches Louisiana, the Mississippi is wider and carries more water than it did in Minnesota.

The land area that a river drains is called a watershed. All the runoff, streams, and rivers of the watershed flow into the same body of water, which could be a larger stream, a lake, or the ocean. The Mississippi drains almost all the land between the Rocky Mountains and the Appalachian Mountains.

Rivers and Ecosystems

Rivers contain many **ecosystems.** The age, flow, and water quality of a river define the type of ecosystem that is formed. Fast-moving

Minnesota. The Mississippi's many tributaries add to its flow. The largest tributaries are the Illinois, the

Old, slow-moving rivers, like the Saranac River in New York, wind across the land. ▶

streams provide excellent homes for trout. The water is quick and clear and has little plant life.

Slow-moving rivers often carry soil and silt. The water is murky. Water plants grow along the banks. Slow-moving rivers can also form **deltas.**

The Mississippi River and Africa's Nile River deltas have many small islands that become new wetland ecosystems. The islands support plant and animal life, including reeds and water grasses, as

? WORDS TO KNOW . . .

deltas (DEL-tuhz) deposits of silt, sand, and gravel at the mouth of a river

well as shellfish, waterbirds, and wading birds.

Fish and water plants that live near a river's source may be different from living things farther downstream. The Colorado River begins high in the Rocky Mountain forests. It rushes through desert in Utah, Nevada, and Arizona. It ends as a stream trickling into the Gulf of California. The trout of the upper Rockies differ greatly from the catfish of southwestern Arizona.

Lakes and Ponds

Lakes and ponds are still water, as opposed to the running water found in rivers and

streams. Land completely surrounds lakes and ponds. The difference between lakes and ponds is the same as the difference between rivers and streams: Lakes are simply larger ponds.

Although lake water doesn't flow like river water, it does move. Wind affects lakes of all sizes. Wind pushes the water, forming waves. Large lakes, such as Europe's Caspian Sea and North America's Lake Superior, may have huge waves that can sink ships. Wave action mixes and moves lake water.

Seasonal changes also move lake water. In autumn, surface water cools and sinks. Top layers of water trade places with bottom layers. This action is called turnover.

◄ Canada's Lake Louise is one of the most beautiful lakes in North America.

PROFILE: LAKE NATRON

Lake Natron in Tanzania, Africa, has an incredibly foul smell. The lake supports few plants and animals. Algae, brine shrimp, and insects somehow survive vile Lake Natron water.

The lake lies just south of the equator, where afternoon temperatures can soar to 150° Fahrenheit (66° Celsius). In that heat, water evaporates quickly. Little rain falls in the area. Underground hot springs full of sodium carbonate refill the lake. The water is caustic. It burns or eats away human and animal flesh.

Flamingos are the only large animals that wade in Lake Natron without suffering burns. Flamingos feast on algae and brine shrimp without fear of predators. No predators dare risk the stinging waters of Lake Natron.

> **? WORDS TO KNOW . . .**
> **algae (AL-jee)** simple, one-celled plants

13

Lakes can hold freshwater, salt water, or alkali water. The Great Lakes are freshwater lakes. The Great Salt Lake in Utah and the Dead Sea are salt lakes. Lake Natron in Africa is an alkali, or soda, lake.

Rivers and Lakes around the World

Rivers and lakes are found on every continent. Even frozen Antarctica has freshwater in places beneath the glacial ice. Bodies of freshwater nourish plants and animals alike, including humans.

Most of Africa's freshwater collects in eight river **basins**: the Nile, Congo/Zaire, Niger, Zambesi, Limpopo, Kasai, Orange, and Volta. Africa's Congo/Zaire River is the only river in the world that flows both north and south of the equator. At 4,145 miles (6,669 kilometers), the Nile is the world's longest river. There are two branches of the Nile—the Blue Nile and the White Nile. The Blue Nile is fed by Lake T'ana in Ethiopia. Lake Victoria, Africa's largest lake, serves as headwaters of the White Nile.

Asia's rivers provide freshwater for earth's most populated region. China's largest rivers are the Yangtze (3,720 miles or 5,985 km) and the Huang, or Yellow, River

WATCH IT!

Discover the story of cichlids, the amazing fish of Lake Tanganyika, Africa, in National Geographic's *Lake Tanganyika: Jewel of the Rift* [ASIN: 0792241525]. The video features fabulous photography and music, along with a truly interesting story.

? WORDS TO KNOW . . .

basins (BAY-suhnz) areas of land around a river from which water drains into the river

◄ The T'is Isat Falls drain Ethiopia's T'ana Lake into the Blue Nile River.

(2,903 miles or 4,671 km). The Huang is called China's Sorrow because its floods have killed millions of people. The Mekong River, a major Asian river, begins in China, and flows through Thailand, Laos, Kampuchea, and Vietnam.

India's main rivers include the Brahmaputra and the

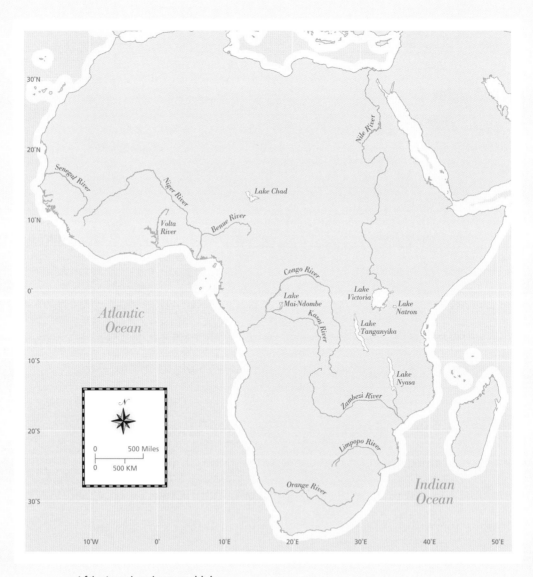

▲ Africa's major rivers and lakes

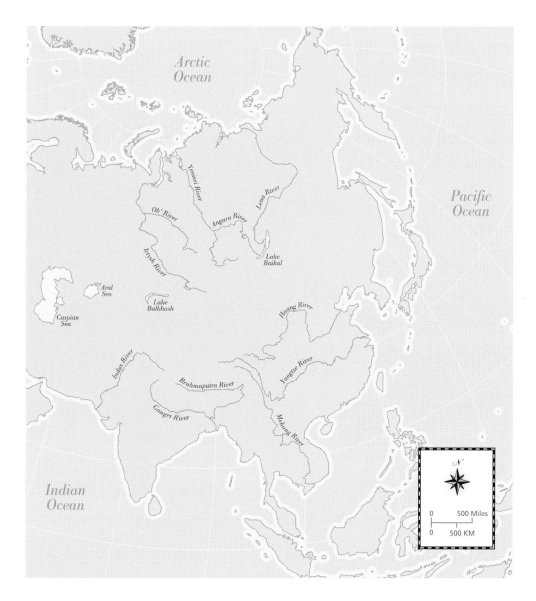

▲ Asia's major rivers and lakes

Ganges. The Brahmaputra River starts on the Tibetan Plateau in China. It passes through the Himalayan Mountains and eastern India before joining the Ganges River in Bangladesh. The Ganges is India's sacred river.

Millions of people believe its waters carry divine powers.

Lake Baikal in Asian Russia is considered the oldest lake on earth. Scientists think the lake has existed for more than 25 million years. It is certainly the deepest lake. Baikal plunges 5,314 feet (1,620 meters) into the ground. That's more than 1 mile (1.6 km) deep!

Australia has more dry rivers than wet ones. Many riverbeds lie empty until heavy rains come—perhaps once a year or once every 10 years. Flash floods rush through the riverbeds. The water empties into rivers, seas, or oceans, and then the bed is dry again. The continent's largest "wet" river is the Murray/Darling **river system** in southeast Australia.

Australia also has many dry lakes. The world's largest dry salt lake is Lake Eyre. It covers 3,254 square miles (8,428 sq km). In the past 100 years, Lake Eyre has held water only three times. The most appropriately named dry lake is Lake Disappointment. It lies in Australia's western desert and undoubtedly disappointed many travelers hoping to find water.

South America's great rivers lie east of the Andes Mountains. The Amazon, the world's second longest

> **? WORDS TO KNOW . . .**
>
> **river system (RIV-ur SISS-tuhm)**
> a major river and its tributaries

river, begins as a stream in the Andes. Hundreds of tributaries pour into the Amazon, including the Madeira, the Purus, and the Rio Negro. The Plata-Paraná river system ranks as the world's seventh largest river. It passes through Brazil, Paraguay, and Argentina

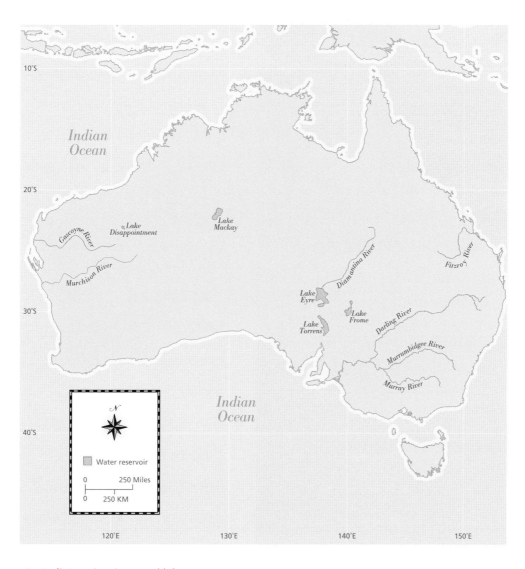

▲ Australia's major rivers and lakes

PROFILE: SOUTH AMERICAN WATERFALLS

South America claims two stunning waterfalls. The world's tallest waterfall—Angel Falls (3,212 feet or 979 m)—spills into the Orinoco River in Venezuela. The Iguazú Falls (above) are short by comparison. They are just 237 feet (72 m) high. However, the falls stretch across 2 miles (3 km) of the Argentina/Brazil border. They make up in width what they lack in height.

before emptying into the Atlantic Ocean.

Many great rivers carve North America's lands. The Mississippi/Missouri system is the largest. In Canada, the Yukon, Mackenzie, and Fraser rivers flow in the west. In the east, Canada and the United States share the Saint Lawrence River. In the southwest, the Rio Grande marks the border between the United States and Mexico.

Canada and the United States also share the Great Lakes—Superior, Michigan, Huron, Erie, and Ontario. Man-made locks and canals connect the Great Lakes to the Saint Lawrence River, which flows into the Atlantic Ocean. The Saint Lawrence Seaway is one of the busiest shipping lanes in the world.

Europe's rivers and lakes have endured difficult conditions due to pollution and over-population. Rivers such as the Danube and the Rhone pass through many countries. Getting those countries to work together for cleaner water has

▲ South America's major rivers and lakes

not always been successful. Factory waste, shipping, and large human populations place heavy demands on rivers. The problems challenging European rivers and lakes are the same for freshwater resources around the world.

▲ North America's major rivers and lakes

▲ Europe's major rivers and lakes

Overcrowded riverbanks damage Asia's Yangtze and Huang rivers as much as they do Europe's Rhine. Pollution in the Ganges is far worse than in the Volga or Danube. Problems are many, but solutions are few and expensive.

📖 **READ IT!**

Take a look at author Steve Parker's *Eyewitness: Pond & River* (DK Publishing, 2000). Learn about freshwater ecosystems, from fish to frogs, plants to pollution.

Focus on Key Species

In the quiet woods of New York's Adirondack Mountains, a beaver family sets to work. The adults gnaw a 4-inch (10-centimeter) tree trunk. They bring down the birch tree in about 15 minutes. Next comes the hard work.

The beavers strip the branches from the trunk and drag them to a stream. They are building their lodge across the fast-flowing mountain

water. The tree's leaves, twigs, and bark provide their food. They use tree trunks, limbs, mud, and rocks to build their home. Their building skills are so good that even a stick or two of dynamite would barely dent a beaver's dam.

Keystone Species

A keystone species is an animal or plant that is vital for the survival of an ecosystem. The species may change the land or create new habitats. Or the species may be the main food of habitat predators. Keystone species of rivers and lakes are beavers, salmon, **copepods,** and **phytoplankton.**

Beaver lodges and dams change water flow and create ponds and marshes. What was once rushing water becomes still water. Animals and plants that cannot live in fast-flowing stream water take advantage of the beavers' efforts. Cattails, wild irises, lilies, reeds, bulrushes, and water grasses spring up. The new plant life attracts insect and bird species.

In the North American west, salmon is a keystone river species. About 140 different animal species depend on salmon for survival. Important species that feed on salmon

 **WATCH IT!**

Beavers are among nature's best engineers. They are always busy, always building, and always interesting. Discover their fascinating lives in the video *Beavers* [ASIN: B00003XAMO].

? **WORDS TO KNOW . . .**

copepods (KOH-puh-pahdz) small water animals related to shrimp that are the main food of many small fish, reptiles, and insects

phytoplankton (FIE-toe-PLANGK-tuhn) one-celled floating water plants, such as algae or diatoms

◄ Beavers gnaw tree trunks and strip branches to build dams strong enough to block raging rivers.

BEAVERS IN THE NEWS

Two conservation groups in Great Britain plan to reintroduce beavers to Scotland. They will place four Norwegian beaver families, each with a male, a female, and three kits, in the Knapdale Forest of Argyll, Scotland. Beavers have not lived in Great Britain for 400 years.

In the 1500s, beavers were prized for their thick fur. The species was hunted to extinction in the British Isles. This event will mark the first time a native species extinct in Great Britain is reintroduced there.

include grizzly bears, otters, and bald eagles. The young salmon feed off adult salmon **carcasses.** Dead salmon also release **nutrients** into the water. River plants feed and thrive on the nutrients provided by rotting salmon.

The health of a lake ecosystem depends on tiny plants and animals called phytoplankton and copepods. Phytoplankton feed young fish, insect **larvae,** and dozens of other animal species. Copepods are tiny animals that are part of the **zooplankton.** Some are not even as large as the head of a pin. They eat phytoplankton, insect larvae, and fish eggs. In turn, copepods are the basic food, or first link, in the animal food chain.

Tiny plankton are a basic food for ▸ fish, reptiles, amphibians, and small mammals.

They feed water insects, wading birds, and mature fish.

Without phytoplankton and copepods, fish, birds, and water mammals could not exist. These **microscopic** animals and plants are the basic elements of life in freshwater.

Umbrella Species

Governments pass laws to protect **endangered** or **threatened** plants and animals. Legal protection stops

? WORDS TO KNOW . . .

endangered (en-DAYN-jurd) close to extinction; few members of a species still surviving

microscopic (mye-kruh-SKOP-ik) too small to be seen with the naked eye; only seen with the help of a microscope

threatened (THRET-uhnd) at risk of becoming endangered

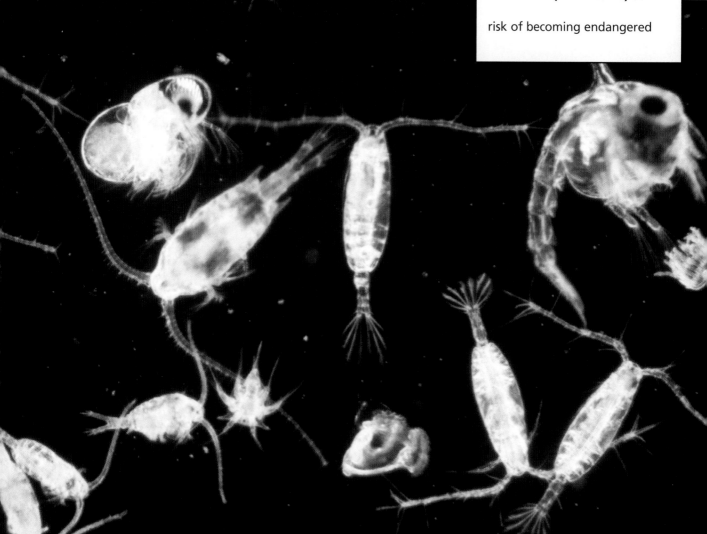

Protecting manatees like this mother and calf helps protect other creatures in their habitat.

📖 **READ IT!**

Life in a River (Lerner Press, 2003) by Valerie Rapp is an Ecosystems in Action book. Follow the Columbia River from its source to the sea, through several ever-changing ecosystems.

people from hunting an animal or digging up or cutting down a plant. With rivers and lakes, laws may limit boats, fishing, building, or human use.

An umbrella species is a protected animal or plant that spreads its legal protection over other creatures. Manatees travel through rivers, feeding on sea grass or water hyacinths. They need protection from speedboats, fishing nets, and pollution. Laws establish areas in which boats can travel only at slow speeds or not at all. Other fish, reptiles, and amphibians that live in the river share the manatees' protection. Reduced river traffic and pollution-free water helps all river beings— not just manatees.

Umbrella species may live in or near lakes and rivers. If they feed in freshwater, their food sources must be protected along with their habitats. Bald eagles are an umbrella species of freshwater biomes.

Bald eagles were once an endangered species. Their populations dropped during the late 1940s and early 1950s. Scientists found that

DDT, a chemical compound used to kill insects, reduced bald eagle populations.

Bald eagles are at the top of their food chain. They eat fish, such as salmon and trout, which feed on smaller fish. Small fish ate the bodies of

Bald eagles require pollution-free ▶
rivers and lakes to survive.

▲ This eagle has made a catch! It is fish for dinner tonight.

Some eggs hatched young with birth defects.

Protection for bald eagles was not protection of the eagles' territory. It was protection from DDT. The eagles gained an advantage because DDT was banned and therefore no longer poisoned insects. Other species that might have eaten DDT-poisoned food shared that benefit.

Piping plovers are another example of an umbrella species in a freshwater biome. Plovers are shorebirds that breed on the sand dunes of Lake Michigan. There are only a few dozen nesting pairs left in the area. The plovers share their territory with sandhill cranes, herons, bufflehead ducks, and turtles. Scientists want to

insects killed by DDT. The chemicals stayed in the insects and fish, and eventually ended up being eaten by eagles. DDT caused eagles to lay eggs with weak shells. Eggs broke when eagles sat on them to brood.

protect the piping plover's habitat. In doing so, they will also protect the plovers' neighbors.

Flagship Species

Flagship species are species that attract the public's attention. Salmon, beavers, whooping cranes, and bald eagles are flagship species of freshwater environments.

The problems faced by flagship species become public issues. When a flagship species

▲ Protecting the nesting areas of migrating birds like the great blue heron will help preserve wading bird species.

▲ This osprey is scanning a nearby lake for fish. It uses its sharp talons to scoop prey from just beneath the water's surface.

makes news, politicians take notice. Laws to protect flagship species also protect other species and ecosystems.

Consider the situation with bald eagles. They were not the only species damaged by DDT. Other birds of prey, such as American peregrine falcons, osprey, and vultures, also suffered. However, the bald eagle is a national symbol of the United States. Politicians had more interest in saving bald eagles than vultures. Laws passed to protect bald eagles saved the vultures, too.

Indicator Species

🦎 Indicator species measure the health of an ecosystem. Many species indicate, or show,

The presence of blue damselflies indicates that this pond provides a healthy habitat. ▶

problems in that ecosystem. Pollution, overbuilding, erosion, and overhunting or overfishing change ecosystems. Indicator species measure those changes.

Insects make excellent indicator species. They quickly die or fail to produce young in unhealthy situations. One way to check if a local pond is healthy is to count the number of dragonflies or damselflies hovering in the air. If there are few or no dragonflies, the pond is

▲ Mussels are filter feeders. When pollution is high in a stream, mussels will die.

🖱 **LOOK IT UP!**

Visit a dragonfly pond! Find out about the plants and animals living around a small pond at *http://www.units.muohio.edu/ dragonfly/index.htmlx.*

too polluted to support life.

Mussels serve as indicator species in many rivers. Mussels are filter feeders. To eat, they filter food and water through their bodies. When there is too little food or too much pollution, mussel colonies die off. If the water is healthy and food is plentiful, mussel colonies grow.

Chapter Three

Predators

❧ Along the Amazon River of South America, a giant river otter swims in a quick, tight spiral. The faster the water moves, the tighter the water swirls. The movement creates a whirlpool that sucks fish from the river muck below. The otter grabs its prey in its paws. It eats the entire fish, head first. Otters use this whirlpool trick to enjoy an easy catch.

Giant otters need about 10 pounds (4.5 kilograms) of food each day. Their favorite meal is catfish, but they also

▲ When this giant otter finishes its meal, it will go hunting again.

Peru's Giant River Otter Project identifies otter habitats and observes otters in the wild. The giant river otter is just one of the many species unique to the Amazon River (below) and its tributaries. Project scientists found mercury pollution in several sites where giant river otters feed. The scientists are trying to reduce pollution in otter habitats. As they study the otters, scientists can decide what is needed to preserve the species.

eat crayfish and frogs. They hunt, eat, and rest throughout the day. Although otters live in burrows on land, they hunt in the water. They are active, aggressive freshwater predators.

Predators of Every Size

Freshwater predators come in all sizes and shapes. The tiniest is the copepod, which is both predator and prey. Large predators include brown bears, otters, crocodiles, alligators, and water snakes. Predators live beside and in the water. They hunt from both above and under water. They crawl, slither, fly, swim, and pounce.

Mammals are the largest predators. Brown bears fish

while salmon are **spawning.** The rest of the time, they eat land animals and plants. River otters and weasels hunt for fish, frogs, beavers, shrews, and muskrats. Although they catch their food under water, they usually eat their catches on land or while floating on their backs in the water.

Reptiles sun themselves on riverbanks in most warm, freshwater regions. They usually live on land, but crocodiles and alligators spend as much time in the water as on solid ground. These dangerous hunters glide through water almost unseen. They quickly seize prey and kill it in their powerful jaws. Yet mother crocodiles transport their young in their mouths without leaving a scratch.

The world's largest snake is also a water predator. The anaconda of South America lurks among the reeds at the water's edge. Anacondas eat wild pigs, deer, fish, other reptiles, and even jaguars. They eat prey whole. Their bodies digest skin, bones, and fur.

Birds That Fish

🐇 Some birds swoop out of the sky, talons stretched, and scoop up trout for dinner. Others bob along on the water, waiting for a meal to swim by. Then they dive down

👁 **WATCH IT!**

Crocodiles: Here Be Dragons (ASIN: 6304474598) gives viewers a close-up look at Nile crocodiles and their lives as fierce predators and gentle parents.

❓ **WORDS TO KNOW . . .**

spawning (SPAWN-ing) producing eggs or young

PROFILE: THE NILE CROCODILE

Nile crocodiles can bring down wilde-beests or zebras with no trouble. They attack lions and water buffaloes. A Nile crocodile's jaws can break a man's leg in two with one bite. In fact, Nile crocs cause more human deaths than lions, tigers, or rhinos.

Nile crocodile hatchlings must hide from predators. For their first few years, they are preyed upon by male crocodiles, birds, and large fish. It takes about seven years for a crocodile to reach adult age. Adult Nile croco-diles can weigh more than 1,500 pounds (680 kg) and can reach 20 feet (6 m) in length. Only humans hunt adult Nile crocodiles.

and snap up prey in their bills. Still others wade into the water and peck at fish, mussels, and worms hiding in the shallows.

Birds of prey rely almost entirely on meat for their diets. Some birds of prey are fish-eaters. Besides bald eagles, African fish hawks and osprey hunt fish. They catch fish while flying, and then return to their nests to eat.

Birds do not have to be birds of prey to be predators. Ducks may upend themselves to hunt snails, mussels, and fish. Other birds dive for their food. Dippers—common around fast-flowing mountain streams in the Rockies and the Andes, as well as in Europe and Asia—dive down to streambeds to find snails

▲ A belted kingfisher dives into a stream in search of food.

and small fish that hide among the rocks. In North and South America, Africa, and Asia, kingfishers perch on overhang- ing branches. When fish swim beneath them, they plunge into the water.

DO IT!

Join a kids' conservation group. The Wildlife Conservation Society has a kids' Web page called Kids Go Wild. You can help save wildlife. Go to *http://www.KidsGoWild.com* to find out how to join.

Cranes, egrets, herons, and flamingos are wading birds. Their long legs allow them to walk through shallow water in search of small fish, shellfish, and insects. The shape of their bills suits the type of food the birds eat. Bills can be spoon-shaped, thin and straight, or curved. A spoonbill scoops up its food. Cranes and egrets peck with long, sharp bills.

▲ Flamingos use bony plates in their mouths to strain their food from the water.

Flamingos have bony plates in their mouths. They suck water through the plates. Their beaks close, and they push out excess water. They feed on brine shrimp, worms, and insects trapped in their mouth plates.

Fishing Fish

🐟 Although some fish feed on plants, most are meat eaters. They prey on insects, eggs, larvae, and smaller fish species. The size of a

◄ African crowned cranes wade into the shallows looking for prey.

predator fish does not relate to the size of its prey. Some fish prey on tiny zooplankton and still grow remarkably large. The pirarucu of South America feeds only on larvae and eggs. Adult pirarucus measure about 13 feet (4 m) long and weigh up to 440 pounds (200 kg).

Large fish, such as pike, trout, and salmon, form the top of the fish food chain in rivers and lakes. Pike, in particular, are aggressive hunters. They often devour all smaller fish from ponds or lakes.

Catfish and carp may feed along river or lake bottoms. They eat dead animals and solid animal waste.

> **? WORDS TO KNOW . . .**
>
> **fry (FRYE)** the young of a fish species

Garbage feeders play an important role in keeping freshwater clean.

Bottom of the Food Chain

At the bottom of the food chain are creatures that are both predators and prey. Copepods, insect larvae, and fish **fry** munch on one another. They are also food for larger fish, frogs, and waterbirds. There is always something larger that will eat the smaller animals of a biome.

Numbers of a certain species make a difference between destruction and survival for predators. A dozen otters hunt in a mountain lake. They each eat quantities

▲ Catfish are bottom feeders. They keep river water clean by eating dead animals and animal waste.

▲ River otters are excellent swimmers. They catch fish in the water but eat their meals on land.

of fish and frogs every day. A 40-pound (18-kg) otter might eat four fish and three frogs in one day, or approximately 1,500 fish and 1,100 frogs per year. Thousands of fish and frogs live in the lake. However, if there were 100 otters, there might not be enough food available to feed them.

Chapter Four

Prey

A lake trout hunts in the shallows of Lake Superior. It can grow to be up to 45 inches (114 cm) long and can weigh about 40 pounds (18 kg). Most people would not consider lake trout prey. They are usually the eaters, not the eaten.

As the trout feeds, a dangerous parasite approaches.

It is the lamprey eel, a creature with no jaws. Lamprey mouths are round and filled with sharp teeth.

The lamprey attaches its mouth to the trout's side. It clings to the trout while it sucks the fish's blood. The lamprey feeds off the trout for a couple of days. Unfortunately for the trout, the lamprey will suck its life away.

▲ Lamprey eels prey upon lake trout like this one from Lake Superior.

▲ This carp doesn't stand a chance for survival once a lamprey eel attaches itself to the carp's body.

Prey by the Numbers

↩ The largest group of prey is made up of the smallest-sized prey. It's a matter of how many prey must be eaten to make a full meal. A predator may fill up on one frog or two dozen tadpoles or 3,000 frog eggs.

The smallest and most numerous prey are zooplankton. The word *plankton* comes from the Greek *planktos,* which means "wandering." Plankton doesn't actually wander. It drifts.

Zooplankton includes copepods and the eggs or young of larger animals.

Copepods are the most common kind of zooplankton. Twelve thousand small copepods weigh in at about 1 ounce (28.3 grams). Dragonfly larvae are considered zooplankton, but an adult dragonfly is not.

Fish and insect species lay eggs by the billions. The chances of any egg reaching adulthood are small. With many species, fewer than three out of one hundred eggs become adults. Generally, the smaller the prey, the larger the number of predators that eat it. Insects, slugs, snails, small fish, worms, birds, lizards, frogs, and larger fish eat eggs. Huge numbers of eggs are necessary if a species is to survive.

PROFILE: EMPEROR DRAGONFLIES

Europe's emperor dragonfly depends on lakes and ponds for producing young. The female makes slits in the leaves of pond weeds above the water. She lays her eggs within the leaves. In three weeks, the eggs hatch, and the larvae drop into the water through the slits.

Now begins a life filled with danger. Dragonfly larvae live in water for two years. They float among the plants in shallow freshwater. They must hide if they are to survive to adulthood. Frogs, carp, otters, shrews, and other insects feed on dragonfly larvae.

After two years of hide-and-seek, the larvae crawl out of the water. They shed their skins. Soft wings emerge. These newly adult dragonflies open their wings to the air. Once the wings dry, the adults can fly.

Building up Defenses

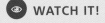 Adult insects and beetles live in an endless cycle of eat-and-be-eaten. Whirligig beetles, for example, eat all day long. They skim across the water's surface, feeding on their favorite food—mosquitoes. Because the whirligig is a surface beetle, it is easy prey for larger insects, birds, and fish. Its defense against predators is to fill surrounding water with a milky-white substance. The beetle then

👁 WATCH IT!

It's not easy being a tadpole or a dragonfly. Learn about these pond creatures in the National Geographic Kids' video *Tadpoles, Dragonflies, and Caterpillars* [ASIN: 6303379184].

▲ Damselfly larvae hide in plain sight. Their green bodies match the plants on which they live.

escapes in the murky water, if it's lucky.

Camouflage hides prey from their enemies. The larvae of blue damselflies are green, like plants. The young shed their skins while holding onto plant stems. Their green color makes them nearly invisible.

Atlantic salmon begin life in rivers or streams. Their coloring for the first year blends with the riverbeds in which they live. After a year, the young salmon change color. They become silver, which provides camouflage while the salmon live at sea.

Other species use poison, hard shells, or sharp spines

? **WORDS TO KNOW . . .**

camouflage (KAM-uh-flahzh)

coloring that blends in with

the surroundings

◄ Whirligig beetles zip across a pond's surface in constant search for insects and larvae.

📖 **READ IT!**

David Josephs' *Lakes, Ponds, and Temporary Pools* (Franklin Watts, 2000) gives readers an appreciation of freshwater life cycles. The information on temporary pools shows how life thrives—even in a puddle.

against their enemies. European backswimmers suck blood from their victims. They poison small insects on surface water. They will also bite and sting predators that come too close. Their stings are painful, even for humans.

Hundreds of species of freshwater mussels survive because of their hard shells. The shells protect them from many possible predators, but not all. Muskrats, raccoons, and herons have no trouble cracking mussel shells to eat the meat inside.

Sharp spines are the only protection the stickleback fish has from predators. The spines ward off smaller fish, but sticklebacks still have predators. Water shrews, otters, storks, and herons feed on sticklebacks. The spines are too small to bother these large hunters.

◀ Raccoons are the neatest eaters. They like to wash their food in a stream before eating.

▲ An infant snapping turtle bursts from its shell.

Other Prey

🐊 Reptiles, amphibians, and rodents are common prey in rivers and lakes. Many are victims only as hatchlings or young. This is true for turtle and crocodile hatchlings.

Snapping turtles lay their eggs on land. The female digs a nest and lays 25 to 50 eggs. Raccoons, weasels, and water rats dig up the eggs almost as soon as they are laid. Once the remaining eggs hatch, the hatchlings become prey for crows, hawks, wading birds, bullfrogs, snakes, and other turtles. Of the

❗ **WOULD YOU BELIEVE?**

Some kinds of water shrews carry enough poison in their mouths to kill 200 frogs, toads, or mice. The shrews use the poison to stun the larger prey and to keep them from struggling.

▲ Water shrews have poison in their saliva. One nip, and their prey will die.

female's 50 original eggs, only three will reach adulthood. As adults, however, snapping turtles have few enemies. They are defenseless only when very young.

Other animals remain small, even as adults, and fall prey to larger animals throughout their lives. Water shrews never weigh more than 1 ounce (28.3 g). They spend their lives avoiding predators.

Water rodents are common river creatures. Water voles, for example, build their burrows with underwater entrances.

A water vole munches on a leaf beside an English pond. ▶

Otters prey on water voles throughout the voles' lives. The voles have developed protection from otters. When hunted, they scratch the muck from the bottom of the river. Then they disappear in a cloud of mud.

Some freshwater fish are common prey. European minnows have adapted to life in freshwater. Minnows are tiny cousins of the carp. They eat almost any small prey, and they are eaten by nearly every larger fish.

Cichlids are another prey species. More than 600 different species, including tilapia and gobies, swim tropical lakes and rivers in Africa and South America. Like minnows, they

> **! WOULD YOU BELIEVE?**
>
> The pumpkinseed sunfish, found in eastern North America, preys on its own young. Females lay as many as 35,000 eggs, producing their own food source. Luckily, enough young survive their cannibal parents for the species to continue to exist.

▲ Blue tilapia move in a school in an African lake.

travel in schools and make easy prey.

Every animal that lives in freshwater biomes will at some point become the prey of another species. Alive or dead, every animal feeds others. Prey may be the eggs, infants, or adults of a species. It can also be the **carrion** left once adults die. Nature does not waste good food. If there are nutrients to be had, something will gnaw, suck, or chomp to get them.

The food cycle depends on prey and predators. Without predators, prey would reproduce in massive numbers. Prey populations would soon take over lakes and streams. Predators keep prey population levels in check. This is an example of nature's balance.

Flora

🦎 A tiny plant, barely the size of a fly's eye, grows on the surface of a man-made pond. The plant has two small leaves, a flower, and a root. It is duckweed, and thousands of them cover the pond's surface water.

It is the smallest known plant.

The man-made pond is a **sewage** treatment tank. Minerals in the water fuel duckweed's rapid growth rate. In effect, duckweed drinks sewage water. It feeds on chemicals, such as

> **? WORDS TO KNOW . . .**
>
> **sewage (SOO-ij)** waste products carried by water from factories and homes

▲ Tiny duckweed filters sewage from pond water.

▲ A bullfrog peeps out from beneath a pond's duckweed-covered surface.

phosphates and nitrogen. When the duckweed's job is done, machines called skimmers remove the plants from the water. The "used" duckweed is fed to cattle or farmed fish. The refreshed water is recycled for human use.

River and Lake Plants

🦎 Rivers and lakes support many of the same plants. Water and sunlight provide the fuel for plant survival. Plants combine sunlight and **chlorophyll**

Willow moss grows on the rocks in a rushing stream. ▶

to make food. This process is called photosynthesis.

Plants may be as small as single cells or as large as trees. Single-celled plants called phytoplankton feed hundreds of freshwater animals. Cypress and mangrove trees grow as comfortably in water as maples and oaks do on land. Their roots create a weblike nursery for young fish and reptiles.

The speed and amount of water in a river determine the types of plants found there. A fast-moving stream has fewer plants because plants cannot root in rushing water. Willow moss is one of the few

LOOK IT UP!

Alien plants are plants that arrive from other places. Some become invasive and take over their new homes. They make an interesting science project. Learn more about non-native plants and the efforts to keep them under control. Visit the Maine Department of Environmental Protection's invasive plants links page at *http://www.state.me.us/dep/blwq/topic/invasives/invlink.htm*. Many other states have similar Web sites.

WATER HYACINTHS IN THE NEWS

Lush lilac-colored water hyacinths add delicate beauty to tropical rivers in North America, South America, Asia, Australia, and Africa. This plant, however, is a killer in areas where it is not native.

Water hyacinths develop into thick mats in tropical rivers. They prevent sunlight from reaching below the surface. Few other plants and animals can grow in these waters. Humans cannot travel or fish in rivers clogged by water hyacinths.

Scientists experimented with hyacinth-eating insects in 20 countries with water hyacinth problems. The insects achieved mixed results. New experiments are under way with a water-hyacinth fly recently found in the Amazon River of South America. Meanwhile, water hyacinths grow unchecked.

plants that thrive in rapid streams. The moss clings to rocks to survive.

Slow-moving rivers have more plant life, both in variety and amount. Plants take root along riverbanks or in shallows. Reeds, water grasses, and bulrushes grow along slow rivers. Where river water is particularly quiet, duckweed, hornweed, water hyacinths, and other free-floating plants live.

Water lilies are among the rooted plants that thrive in slow-moving rivers, ponds, and lakes. Water lilies send roots into soft river mud. Their stems stretch through the water to the surface, where leaves and flowers grow.

▲ A dense growth of water lilies prevents needed sunlight from reaching the lake bottom.

Lake Zones

🦎 Freshwater lakes have three life zones. The zones are **littoral, limnetic,** and **profundal.** Plants can live only in the littoral and

▲ Bright green algae cover the entire surface of this pond.

limnetic zones. They do not live in the profundal zone because there is no sunlight.

The littoral zone hosts cattails, reeds, and dozens of other wildflowers, ferns, grasses, and trees. The limnetic zone is home to phytoplankton. The green slime floating on still ponds is usually a type of phytoplankton called algae.

Some plants live mostly below the water's surface. Bladderwort, for example, survives under water by trapping and eating insects and larvae. The plant has bladders, or air pockets, that keep the branches upright. Bladderwort sends shoots above the surface only when it is time to flower.

Surviving Winters

Water plants in **temperate** zones adjust to weather changes that come with winter. When water temperatures drop, ice may form on the surface, blocking sunlight. Some plants simply sink to the lake's bottom in winter. They lie **dormant** until spring weather warms the surface water. Water starworts and frogbit are winter sleepers.

Other water plants drop their leaves. Water lily leaves fall each autumn. The plant stores food in its roots. Spring brings new leaf growth and flowers to produce seeds.

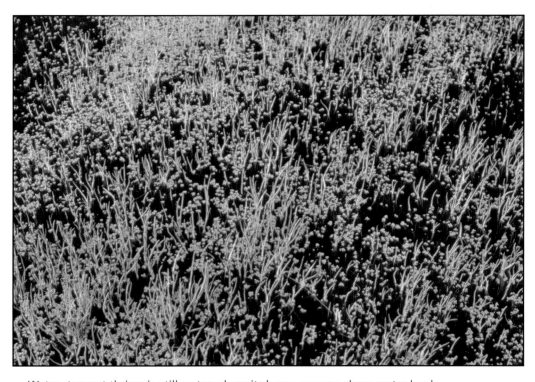

▲ Water starwort thrives in still water where its leaves emerge above water level.

Chapter Six

Herbivores

🦢 A family of black swans glides across a still pond. The cob (male) and pen (female) mate for life. Their young, called cygnets, swim behind their parents.

Black swans are native to Australia.

Until swans reach adulthood, they will eat insects and small **invertebrates,** such as slugs, snails, and worms. When they reach adulthood, swans become herbivores—they eat only plants. They browse on grasses along the

❓ **WORDS TO KNOW . . .**

invertebrates (in-VUR-tuh brits)

animals with no backbones

▲ This hippo mother and baby seem to be sharing a joke.

shore. Swans also eat grains such as wild rice, which is a kind of grass, and the roots of water plants.

Plant Eaters in the Water

🐇 Freshwater plant eaters are as varied as meat eaters. The smallest are zooplankton. They eat phytoplankton. The largest freshwater herbivores are dugongs and manatees. These water mammals munch their way through tons of water hyacinth, eelgrass, and sawgrass each year.

Plant eaters perform an important function in the

◄ These black swan mates have built a nest beside a quiet Australian pond.

Zebra mussels are European imports to North America. They arrived in the Great Lakes in the 1980s, probably carried in the water that was in ships. They have been a problem there ever since. They reproduce more quickly than native North American mussels and freshwater clams. Zebra mussels are "muscling" the locals out of existence.

In a space slightly larger than 1 square yard (.8 sq m), scientists counted 1,000 zebra mussels. Within six months, the population had exploded. That same area had 700,000 mussels.

Zebra mussels eat available phytoplankton. They reduce food for other species, such as freshwater shrimp. Where zebra mussel populations continue to grow, the populations of native shellfish have dropped to zero.

freshwater food web. They take in plant nutrients, which collect in their bodies. As they digest the plants, the plant matter turns into energy. Animals that eat herbivores also benefit from the plant energy and nutrients stored in their prey.

Hundreds of varieties of plant-eating snails and mussels hug the river bottoms. Snails thrive on pond slime. They eat algae and rotting plants. Mussels are filter feeders. They take in water and phytoplankton. They strain plant food from the water.

Dining at the Water's Edge

Some waterbirds, such as swans, wigeons, and geese, eat

▲ Snow geese eat mostly plants, seeds, and grains.

mainly plants, seeds, and grains. Others, such as mandarin ducks and pintail ducks, prefer seeds, nuts, and roots. Some ducks also eat insects and shellfish. They are **omnivores.**

Among water mammals, the most common herbivores are rodents. Nutrias, beavers, and capybaras are the largest rodent herbivores. Throughout their lives, their two extended front teeth continue to grow. They gnaw regularly to wear down their front teeth.

> **?** **WORDS TO KNOW . . .**
>
> **omnivores (OM-nuh-vorz)**
> animals that eat both plants
> and meat

▲ This South American nutria resembles a skinny-tailed beaver. Nutrias, however, live in burrows instead of dams.

Nutrias look like thin-tailed beavers. They munch their way through marsh grasses, crops, and just about any plant life near their burrows. They will even eat bald cypress tree bark.

Beavers prefer the young saplings of oak, birch, elm, and other deciduous (leaf-bearing) trees. Beavers waste nothing of the trees they fell.

They eat bark, leaves, roots, and twigs. They also feed on water plants, such as cattails, reeds, and bulrushes.

Capybaras are the world's largest rodents. They live in South America. Capybaras spend most of their days wallowing in mud. They feed on reeds, lilies, grasses, bulrushes, fruit, grains, seeds, and nuts.

Chapter Seven

A Cycle of Life

Salmon gather at the mouth of the Fraser River in Canada. They are driven there by **instinct.** Several years before, these same salmon swam out to sea from this same river. Now, they have returned to breed. Danger lurks for salmon along their journey upstream. At the mouth of the Fraser, orcas and seals attack the **shoals** of salmon.

The Fraser, like many rivers, has dams and hydroelectric

> **?** WORDS TO KNOW . . .
>
> **instinct (IN-stingkt)** a way of acting or doing things that comes naturally to a person or animal
>
> **shoals (SHOLES)** groups of fish

▲ Sockeye salmon head back to the stream where they were born to lay their eggs.

plants along its route. Salmon ladders allow some fish to move upriver past the dams. The ladders are levels of concrete over which water flows. The salmon hurl themselves up each step.

Salmon use scent to tell them the exact place of their birth. This is where they will spawn. Female salmon dig shallow nests in the gravel. These nests, or redds, will be the nursery for her eggs. She may deposit all her eggs in one redd or use several nests.

Female salmon carry between 2,500 and 7,500 eggs. They lay all their eggs in one season. Males swim over the redds and fertilize the eggs. The females then cover the nests with gravel.

◄ A salmon's journey home is a tough one and involves traveling over rapids and salmon ladders beside dams.

The adults usually have only one chance to produce young. Most adult salmon die after they have spawned. Only cutthroat and steelhead salmon live to spawn a second time.

Salmon eggs hatch about 100 days after being laid. The young salmon, called alevin, remain in the redd. They live off their own yolk for a month. Then they must leave the protected nest to find food.

The month-old fry emerge from the nest and immediately search for food. They eat flies and other fish eggs. If carcasses of dead adult salmon lie near them, the fry eat the rotting flesh. The fry hide among water plants and under fallen tree branches. They must feed and grow to about 6 inches (15 cm) long before they can leave the river.

Juvenile salmon, called smolts, will leave the river and travel into the ocean. Their bodies must change so they can survive in salt water. The smolts eat beetles, ants, grasshoppers, and worms. As the smolts journey to the sea, squawfish, pike, loons, herons, and terns prey on them.

Adult salmon travel in huge schools, feeding on copepods, krill, shrimp,

📖 **READ IT!**

Salmon Stream by Carol Reed-Jones (Dawn Publications, 2001) takes readers on the dangerous journey of the salmon cycle of life.

❓ **WORDS TO KNOW . . .**

juvenile (JOO-vuh-nile)

young, not yet having reached adulthood

🖱 **LOOK IT UP!**

Oregon's Riverdale Grade School hosts *The Salmon Page.* Learn everything you need to know about salmon at this Web site: *http://www.riverdale.k12.or.us/salmon.htm.*

▲ Bears prove their skills as fishers when the salmon run on this Alaskan river.

and plankton. They swim in ocean waters hundreds of miles north of the Fraser River.

Most salmon spend from one to seven years at sea. Predators constantly hunt them. Salmon sharks, pol-lock, tuna, cod, sea lions, swordfish, and orcas feast on adult salmon.

Suddenly, the urge to reproduce strikes the sal-mon. They head for their home streams. Far out to sea, they rely on instinct to find their way back. Once they get close to the mouth of the Fraser, they "smell" their way home.

When salmon die, their bodies fulfill a final chore for nature. Grizzly bears, eagles, wolves, foxes, and minks dine on dying salmon. Salmon carcasses rot and feed the soil. They add nutrients to

 DO IT!

Fight water pollution. Encourage your parents to buy biodegradable detergent for laundry, dishes, and washing cars. Most cleaning detergents will kill the grass if you use them outside to wash lawn furniture or the car. Cleaning chemicals and oil also filter into the soil and pollute groundwater.

▲ Bald eagles join the salmon feeding frenzy.

▲ These tiny salmon eggs escaped being eaten. Will they survive to adulthood?

the river and, even in death, feed their own young.

Of the original thousands of eggs laid, only about 2 percent survive to spawn another generation of salmon. This is the salmon cycle of life. More than 140 animal species thrive because of the salmon's curious journey from river to ocean to river again.

Chapter Eight

The Amazing Amazon

A capybara drinks at the water's edge. It is the world's largest rodent, weighing about 80 pounds (36 kg). The capybara spends its days in water. It lives in groups of about

▲ A capybara in the Amazon marshes provides a comfortable resting place for a cattle tyrant bird.

20 other capybaras in the Amazon River marshes.

Many predators lie in wait along the brown, silt-filled Amazon. Capybaras are wary of jaguars, **caimans,** harpy eagles, and large snakes. Today, a snake presents the greatest danger.

An anaconda slips unseen through the reeds. It eats everything from wild pigs to wading birds. Today's menu features capybara.

The capybara has no chance against the anaconda. Adult anacondas stretch 16 feet (4.9 m) long and weigh about 500 pounds (227 kg). In the Amazon River basin, anacondas are top predators. Their only real enemies are humans.

The Greatest River

ᑭ The Amazon River is a massive river system that moves two-thirds of the fresh river water and lake water in the world. The river's volume is five times greater than that of the Mississippi River. The

> **?** **WORDS TO KNOW . . .**
>
> **caimans (KAY-mehnz)** small members of the crocodile family

◄ Amazingly, this anaconda can stretch its jaws to eat a capybara whole.

Amazon carries 10 times more water than the Nile River. The water moves so quickly and with such force that Amazon River silt clouds the ocean water as far as 185 miles (298 km) into the Atlantic.

The Amazon begins as a mere trickle more than 16,250 feet (4,950 m) up in the Andes Mountains. The river falls nearly 16,000 feet (4,877 m) in the first 600 miles (965 km) of its flow. In all, the Amazon runs 3,900 miles (6,275 km). Tributaries of the Amazon collect water from Bolivia, Peru, Venezuela, Colombia, Ecuador, and Brazil. The river's basin covers about 2,700,000 square miles (6,993,000 sq km)—about 10 times the size of Texas.

▲ Look at the difference in the color of the water where the Rio Negro meets the Amazon near Manaus.

More than 10,000 smaller rivers and streams swell the Amazon's waters. The largest tributaries are the Madeira, Purus, Tocantins, Japurá, and the Rio Negro.

❗ WOULD YOU BELIEVE?

The black water of the Rio Negro meets the white water of the Amazon near Manaus, Brazil. For more than 50 miles (80 km), the two waters travel side by side without mixing together.

▲ This oxbow lake formed near where the Jurua River feeds into the Amazon.

Together, they form a network of waterways running through rain forest, grasslands, swamps, and marshes.

The Amazon and its tributaries include white-water, black-water, and clear-water rivers. The main river, the Amazon, is a white-water river. In this case, white-water does not mean filled with rapids for kayaking or water rafting. It means filled with chalky, beige silt. Black-water rivers, such as the Rio Negro, are not really black. Rotting plant matter dyes the water the color of strong tea. The water travels over sandy beds, so it picks up very little silt or soil in it. Black-water rivers are clear, but dark. Clear-water rivers have clean, clear, silt-free water.

Amazon Plants and Animals

The most fascinating aspect of the Amazon basin is the incredible number of plants and animals found there. Scientists have recorded 40,000 different species of flowering plants, along with 10,000 types of trees and grasses. Many Amazon species have not yet been discovered.

The region supports 1,800 types of birds and hundreds of different fish species. There are more than 250 types of mammals, living in both the water and on the surrounding land. The broadest species range is in the insect world. Scientists know there are at least

The Amazon flows through one of the wettest regions of the world. At certain places along the river's route, rainfall measures more than 200 inches (508 cm) a year. Even the drier areas are wet. Yearly rainfall averages 100 inches (254 cm) across the river's full length. Compare that to annual rainfall rates in Los Angeles (15 inches/38 cm) or New York City (42 inches/107 cm).

👁 WATCH IT!

Learn more about the Amazon River and its rain forest. Watch National Geographic's *Amazon: Land of the Flooded Forest* [ASIN: 6304473869].

15,000 species of insects. However, they estimate that number may be as large as 6 million.

Willows, orchids, and cane grass are common. Not quite so common are strangler figs and giant water lilies. Strangler figs begin as seeds high in the branches of a host tree. The figs send roots down to the forest floor. Eventually, the fig kills the host tree. Giant water lilies float in the quiet bends of the Amazon. They can grow as much as 7 feet (2 m) across. The thorny underside wards off herbivores. Giant water lilies are so large that they have been used as boats.

Mammals of the Amazon basin range from screaming howler monkeys to silent

These giant water lilies are so large ▶ that Amazon natives have used them as boats.

jaguars. River dolphins and manatees are the largest water mammals. Both are endangered species.

The region's birds fill the land with color. Scarlet ibis, roseate spoon-

! WOULD YOU BELIEVE?

The world's only aquatic marsupial, the water opossum, lives in the Amazon basin. A marsupial is an animal that carries its young in a pouch.

bills, and jabirus feast on the fish, frogs, and insects along the Amazon's banks. King-fishers dive into the water below in search of cichlids. Jacanas use their long toes to walk on water as they hunt.

Reptiles slink, slither, and slip through murky Amazon waters. Caimans sun them-selves on the riverbanks. They hunt at night, when prey can-not see them approach.

The Amazon has several deadly snakes. Poisonous fer-de-lance snakes slip along waterways and through wet forests. The Amazon's bushmaster is the Western Hemisphere's largest poison-ous snake.

Creatures that do not fear snake venom do fear boas and

▲ Caimans are the smallest members of the crocodile family, but their teeth seem plenty large!

anacondas. They are both constrictors. They squeeze their victims until they suffocate. The Amazon has red-tailed boas, Amazon tree boas, and rainbow boas, as well as two types of anacondas.

Amazon fish feed thousands of people who live in the region. The giant catfish, called the paraiba, makes a tasty barbecue. Needlefish, sole, and smaller catfish are also delicious to eat. One fish that few people want to catch is the piranha. Piranhas usually swim alone. When they do travel in schools, they are fearsome predators. Like sharks, piranhas can smell blood in the water. The scent sends the fish into a feeding frenzy. A school of piranhas can reduce a much larger animal to a pile of bones in mere minutes.

Insects, the largest group of animals in the Amazon, are too plentiful to list. Beetles, flies, ants, termites, and mosquitoes thrive by the billions in the Amazon's warm, wet weather.

The Amazon also supports stunningly beautiful butterflies. The Brazilian morpho butterfly has vivid blue wings on one side and camouflaged browns and yellows on the other. Green long-winged butterflies and Aurorina clear-winged butterflies dance among the shadows of the rain forest.

[Chapter Nine]

The Human Touch

❧ On July 23, 1969, the Cuyahoga River caught fire. The Cleveland, Ohio, fire department quickly put it out. The damage was minor. However, the fact that an American river caught fire shocked the nation.

For hundreds of years, the world's cities used local rivers as sewer connections. Factories poured waste into rivers and lakes by the ton. Storm runoff, complete with chemical pollution, swelled

▲ Today, the Cuyahoga River preserve shows what can be done when a community works for clean water.

streams and rivers.

When the Cuyahoga caught fire, efforts were already under way to clean it up. Within three years, the Clean Water Act of 1972 passed. The new law added government power to saving U.S. waterways.

Thirty years later, the upper Cuyahoga supports 27 species of fish, including bluegill, pike, and bass. The river continues to need work and attention. Still, the current Cuyahoga is vastly cleaner than the 1969 river that *Time* magazine

👁 **WATCH IT!**

Africa's Stolen River (ASIN: 6304473834) records the disappearance of the Savuti Channel of Botswana over seven years. The video portrays the changes animals must make in order to survive when their main water source is lost.

◄ In 1969, the Cuyahoga River, passing through Cleveland, Ohio, actually caught fire!

American Rivers, a group dedicated to preserving and restoring U.S. rivers, has declared 11 rivers endangered:

1. Upper Missouri River (Montana, North Dakota, South Dakota)

2. Big Sunflower River (Mississippi)

3. Klamath River (Oregon, California)

4. Kansas River (Kansas, Missouri)

5. White River (Arkansas)

6. Powder River (Montana, Wyoming)

7. Altamaha River (Georgia)

8. Allagash Wilderness Water-way (Maine)

9. Canning River (Alaska)

10. Guadalupe River (Texas)

11. Apalachicola River (Florida)

described: "Chocolate-brown, oil, bubbling with subsurface gases, it oozes rather than flows."

Threats to Clean Water

In the United States, 40 percent of the nation's fresh-water sources are undrinkable. Throughout Europe, Asia, and Africa, rivers and lakes struggle to refresh themselves. Freshwater problems exist on every continent on which people live.

Major threats come from chemical pollution, overdevel-opment along rivers and lakes, sewage, industrial pollution, and species that are not native to the area. In regions with large rain forests, timber cutting increases erosion and the amount of soil in water. Change in water flow due to man-made dams also takes a serious toll on freshwater fish, snails, and mussels.

Fertilizers and pest killers can be used hundreds of miles away and still affect an ecosystem. Chemicals enter rivers and lakes through runoff or groundwater. Fertilizers encourage the explosive growth of water plants and algae. Pest killers reduce the insect populations that control plant growth. Poison sprayed on Iowa corn could easily end up in the bodies of Louisiana pelicans.

Acid rain is another form of chemical pollution. It comes from burning fossil fuels, such as oil, gas, or coal. Humans use

▲ Pollution pours into a stream from a chemical factory.

fossil fuels to power cars and trucks, heat homes, and run factories. Burned fuel produces **emissions** that contain

> **?** WORDS TO KNOW . . .
>
> **emissions (i-MISH-uhnz)** things that are sent off or out, such as gases

sulfur, nitrogen, and chlorine. These are basic chemical elements found in nature.

When amounts of sulfur, nitrogen, and chlorine combine with elements in the air, they form acid. The acids exist with water vapor in our **atmosphere.** When rain falls, so does the acid.

Historically, people built

▲ Busy river transportation makes maintaining clean water difficult. These barges leak oil, dump trash, and occasionally sink.

▲ Garbage piles up on the banks of Egypt's Nile River.

cities along rivers and lakes. These locations provided easy access to freshwater. Shipping and receiving goods by water was quicker and cheaper than by land. The problem is that a river or lake has only so much water. Draining water from these sources for human use creates problems in which freshwater ecosystems suffer. In addition, huge populations create large amounts of trash

DO IT!

The U.S. Environmental Protection Agency has a series of programs for "adopting" area watersheds. Volunteers work to ensure clean water resources within each state. Look up the program in your state at *http://yosemite.epa.gov/water/adopt.nsf/adopt+forms+by+state?openview.*

▲ Zebra mussels—an alien species in the Great Lakes—are unwanted invaders.

and sewage. Increased facilities that handle trash and sewage have not kept up with growing populations.

In the past, rivers also offered a convenient dumping ground for industrial waste. In many cases, the poisonous nature of waste products remained unknown. People became concerned only when frogs appeared with extra eyes or legs. All that time, human beings had been drinking the same water the frogs were in.

Alien species have become a worldwide problem. These are not fish from Mars or plants from Venus. They are non-native species—animals and plants that may take over their new homes after they arrive from other places. Alien water hyacinth has invaded Australia, Asia, Pacific Islands, and the United States. Zebra mussels, Asian clams, and sea lampreys hitched rides to the Great Lakes on ships.

Once an alien species takes hold, it is hard to contain. Bringing in predators to attack the invaders just creates new problems. What happens when the newly arrived predator gets out of control?

Fifty years ago, England's Thames River was little more than an open sewer. Pollution had killed most fish and water animals in the Thames. The British government began a clean-up effort to restore the river. They built sewage treatment facilities. Laws stopped

GANGES RIVER IN THE NEWS

The Ganges River is holy water to India's many Hindus. It is the main water source for 400 million people. It is also one of the most polluted rivers on earth.

Today, 27 major towns pour raw sewage into the Ganges. Factories dump toxic waste into the water. However, some of this pollution results from Indian death rites. Bodies are cremated, and the remaining ashes are placed in the Ganges. Unfortunately, wood costs a lot of money in India. To save on wood, bodies are only partly cremated. The half-cremated bodies float among sewage and industrial poisons.

factories from dumping waste into the river.

Today, fish swim happily in the Thames. The river is one of the cleanest city rivers in the world. Strictly enforced laws keep the Thames flowing clean and clear.

It would seem logical for humans, who need water to

▲ A family helps keep riverbanks clean by picking up trash.

live, to take care of the world's water supply. Unfortunately, modern society is wasteful. Most people never think that fresh, clean water will run out. Serious efforts are needed to clean rivers and lakes, protect freshwater species, and reduce pollution. Without these efforts, the last drop of fresh water from your faucet may drip sooner than you think.

◄ England's now-beautiful Thames River was once as polluted as a sewer.

Chart of Species

CONTINENT	KEYSTONE SPECIES	FLAGSHIP SPECIES	UMBRELLA SPECIES	INDICATOR SPECIES
AFRICA	phytoplankton, zooplankton, Nile crocodiles, hippopotamuses,	Nile crocodiles, hippopotamuses, crowned cranes, tilapia	cranes, osprey, hippopotamuses	dragonflies, beetles, mussels, oysters, water spiders
ASIA	phytoplankton, zooplankton	Ganges **River dolphins**, gharials, fishing cats, Indus **River dolphins**, river terrapins	cranes, osprey	damselflies, dragonflies, beetles, water spiders
AUSTRALIA	phytoplankton, zooplankton, Murray **cod**, trout **cod, catfish**	platypuses, **dugongs**	dugongs, osprey, platypuses	dragonflies, beetles, mussels, catfish, water spiders
EUROPE	phytoplankton, zooplankton, beavers	salmon, beavers, otters, water voles, kingfishers	great crested grebes, cranes, osprey	dragonflies, damselflies, mussels, beetles
NORTH AMERICA	beavers, salmon, copepods, phytoplankton,	salmon, beavers, whooping cranes, bald eagles, manatees, Eastern spiny softshell turtles	manatees, bald eagles, piping plovers, **cranes, osprey**	dragonflies, damselflies, mussels, catfish
SOUTH AMERICA	phytoplankton, zooplankton, caimans, giant river otters	giant river otters, dugongs, Amazon River dolphins	dugongs, osprey, giant river otters	mussels, beetles, water spiders, dragonflies

▲ The above chart gives a starting point for identifying key species. Each river, stream, lake, and pond environment has its own key species. The above chart lists some of those species.

[Bold-faced entries are the ones discussed in the text.]